HISTORY OF BASEBALL

KENNY ABDO

Fly!
An Imprint of Abdo Zoom
abdobooks.com

abdobooks.com

Published by Abdo Zoom, a division of ABDO, P.O. Box 398166, Minneapolis, Minnesota 55439.

Printed in the United States of America, North Mankato, Minnesota.
052019
092019

Photo Credits: Alamy, AP Images, iStock, Redux Pictures, Shutterstock, ©Keith Allison cover/CC BY-SA 2.0
Production Contributors: Kenny Abdo, Jennie Forsberg, Grace Hansen
Design Contributors: Dorothy Toth, Neil Klinepier

Library of Congress Control Number: 2018963573

Publisher's Cataloging-in-Publication Data

Names: Abdo, Kenny, author.
Title: History of baseball / by Kenny Abdo.
Description: Minneapolis, Minnesota : Abdo Zoom, 2020 | Series: History of sports | Includes online resources and index.
Identifiers: ISBN 9781532127373 (lib. bdg.) | ISBN 9781532128356 (ebook) | ISBN 9781532128844 (Read-to-me ebook)
Subjects: LCSH: Baseball--History--Juvenile literature. | Baseball--Juvenile literature. | Sports--History--Juvenile literature.
Classification: DDC 796.35709--dc23

TABLE OF CONTENTS

BASEBALL

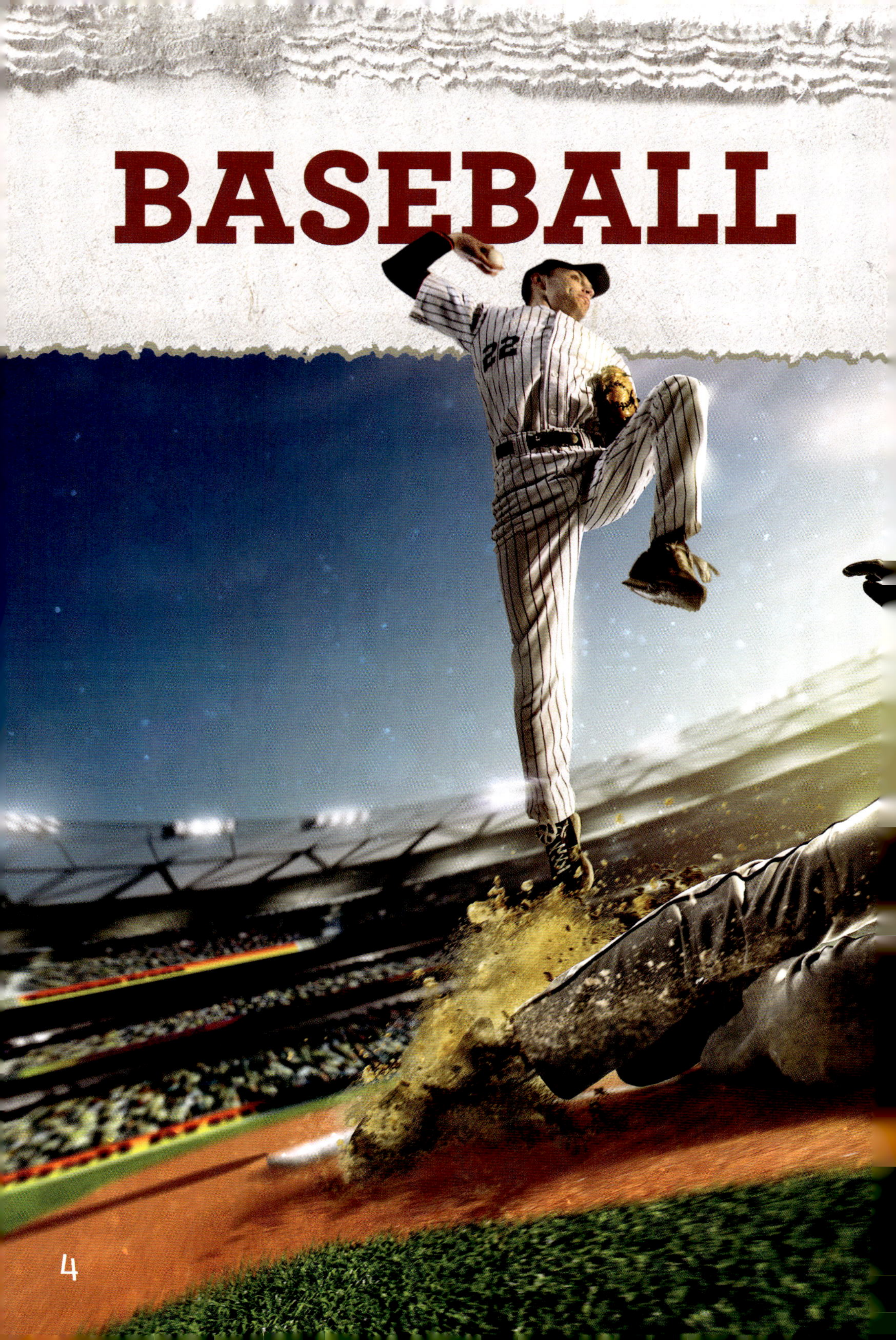

Sliding into homes around the world, baseball is one of the most popular sports in the U.S. and around the world.

Baseball is played between two teams of nine players on an enclosed field. The objective is to score more runs than the **opponent**.

WARM UP

Bat-and-ball games have been around for a long time. No one knows when they were created. It is believed they were first played in the mid 1700s or early 1800s.

FENWAY PARK
1916
1918
1946
1967
1975
1986

Baseball became the "national pastime" of the United States in the mid-1850s. The oldest ballpark still in use is Fenway Park in Boston, Massachusetts. It opened in 1912. It is older than both the Jefferson and Lincoln Memorials.

THRILL

Baseball is fun for all ages. The youngest pitcher in Major **League** Baseball (MLB) history is Joe Nuxhall. He was just 15 years old when he first played for the Cincinnati Reds. Derek Jeter was 40 when he became the oldest player to have more than two hits during an **All-Star Game**.

The first MLB game aired on television in 1939. It was a **doubleheader** between the Brooklyn Dodgers and the Cincinnati Reds. The Dodgers won, 6 to 1.

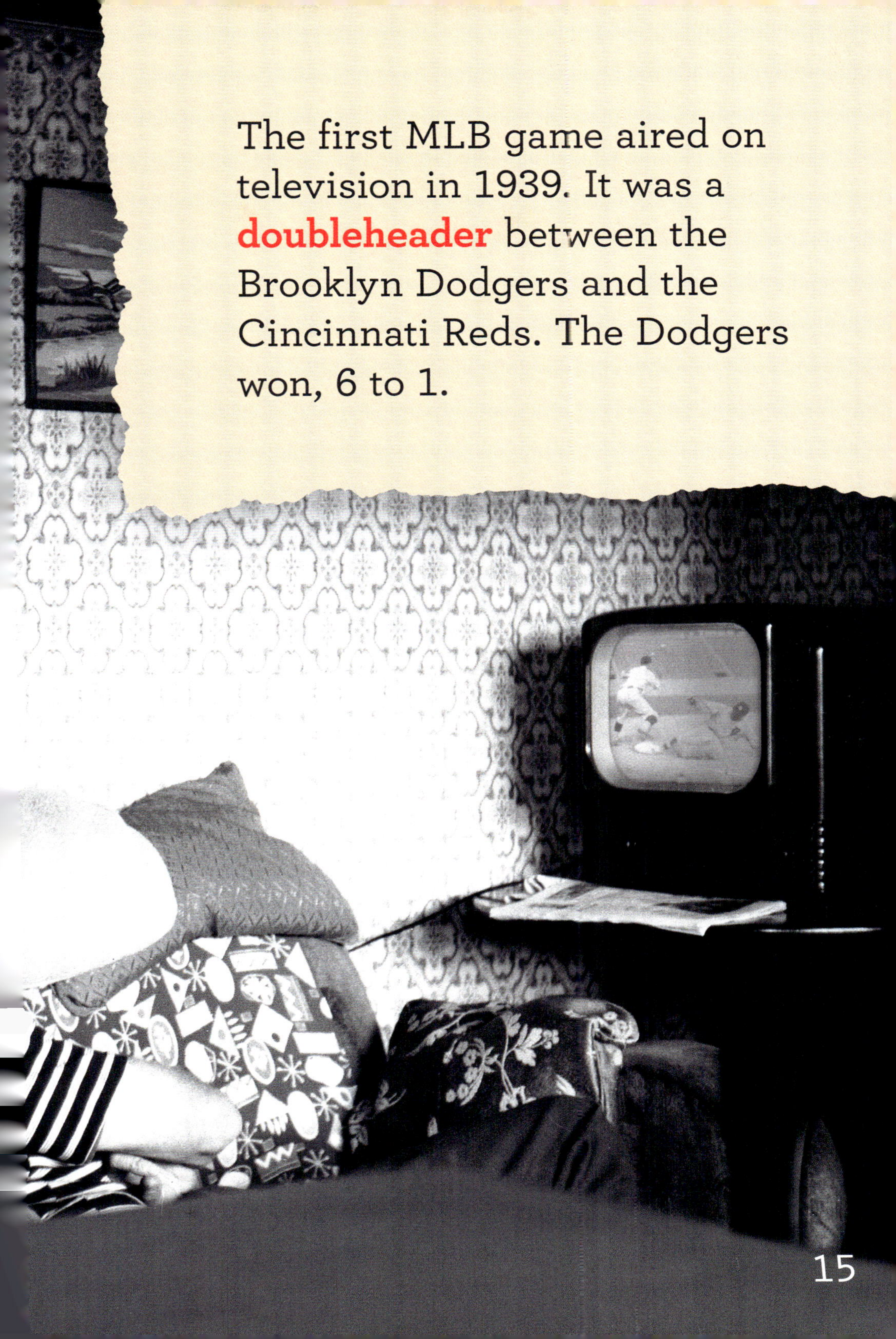

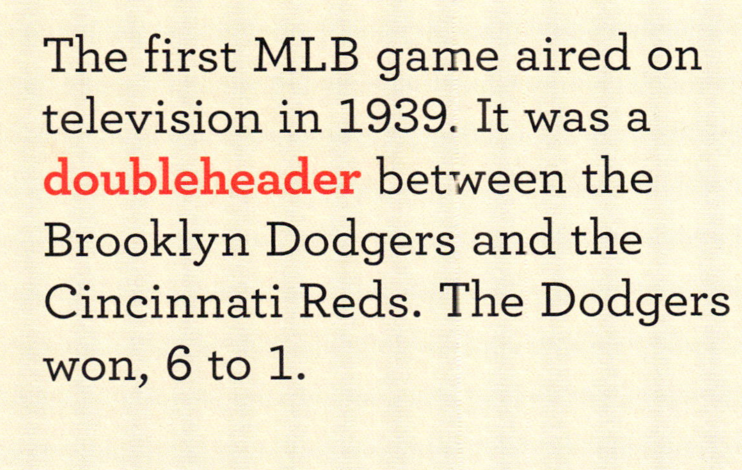

BIG SHOW

Baseball games will go as long as they need to. The longest was between the Milwaukee Brewers and the Chicago White Sox in 1984.

The game was called off after more than 8 hours of play across two days!

Omega
Quaker Oats
WILSON WHISKEY
HOOT MON!
C.M.C.
GARTERS FOR MEN
HOSE SUPPORTERS FOR
EMERSON SHOE
BASE B

The **World Series** is the **championship** series of the MLB that happens every year. A team from the American **League** (AL) and National League (NL) play in a best-of-seven playoff. The Boston Americans won the first World Series in 1903.

The Boston Red Sox beat the Los Angeles Dodgers in five games to win the 2018 **World Series**. The two teams played each other for the same **title** more than 100 years earlier. It is the longest gap between World Series meetings in MLB history.

GLOSSARY

All-Star Game – a yearly game played by the best players from the American (AL) and National league (NL).

championship – a game held to find a first-place winner.

doubleheader – two games played by the same teams back-to-back.

league – a group of teams that compete against each other.

opponent – a rival team.

title – a first-place position in a contest.

World Series – a series of games, where the team who wins a best-of-seven playoff is determined champions of the year.

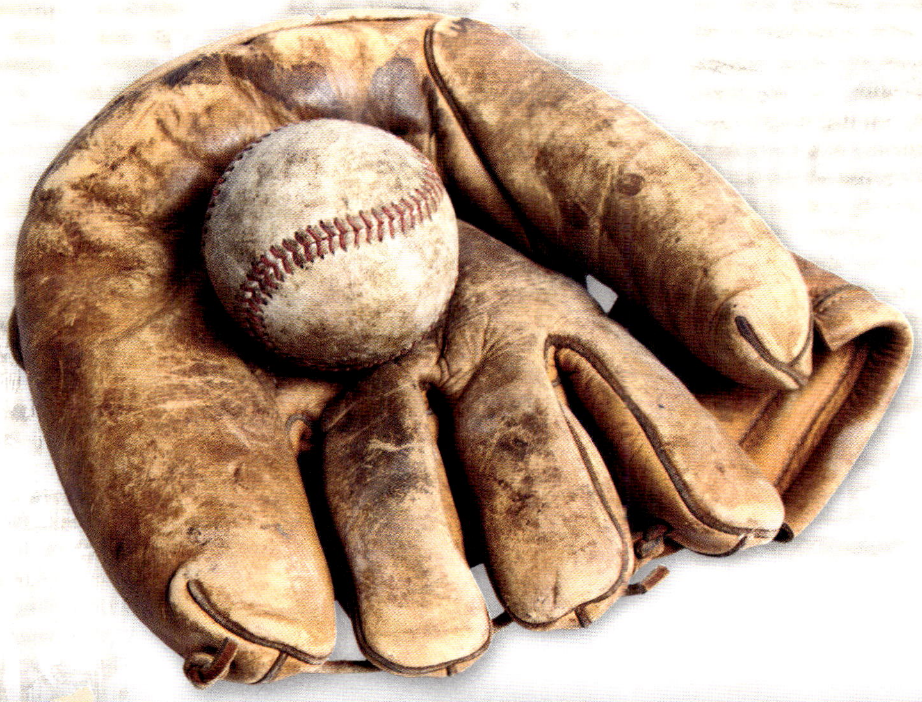

ONLINE RESOURCES

To learn more about baseball, please visit **abdobooklinks.com** or scan this QR code. These links are routinely monitored and updated to provide the most current information available.

INDEX